We Work at the
Vet's

Angela Aylmore

Heinemann Library
Chicago, Illinois

Customer Service   888-454-2279
Visit our website at www.heinemannlibrary.com

Photo research by Erica Newbery
Designed by Jo Hinton-Malivoire and bigtop
Printed in China by South China Printing Company

10 09 08 07 06
10 9 8 7 6 5 4 3 2 1

Library of Congress Cataloging-in-Publication Data
Aylmore, Angela.
  We work at the vet's / Angela Aylmore.
      p. cm. -- (Where we work)
  Includes bibliographical references and index.
   ISBN 1-4109-2245-6 (library binding - hardcover) -- ISBN 1-4109-2250-2 (pbk.)
  1. Veterinary medicine--Juvenile literature. 2. Veterinarians--Juvenile literature. I. Title. II. Series.
  SF756.A95 2006
  636.089--dc22

                        2005033386

Acknowledgments
The publishers would like to thank the following for permission to reproduce photographs:
Alamy p. **15** (Network Photographers Ltd); Ardea pp. **4–5** (John Daniels), **19** (John Daniels); Corbis p. **6–7** (Royalty Free), **8** (Tom Stewart); Getty Images p. **14** (Photodisc); Holt Studios p. **16**; Naturepl.com p. **9** (T J Rich); Photolibary pp. **10–11** (Creatas); Rex Features pp. **12–13**, **21**. Quiz pp. **22–23**: **astronaut** (Getty/Photodisc), **brush and comb** (Corbis/DK Limited), **doctor** (Getty Images/Photodisc), **firefighter helmet** (Corbis), **ladder** (Corbis/Royalty Free), **scrubs** (Corbis), **space food** (Alamy/Hugh Threlfall), **stethoscope** (Getty Images/Photodisc), **thermometer** (Getty Images/Photodisc).

Cover photograph of a vet reproduced with permission of Corbis.

Every effort has been made to contact copyright holders of any material reproduced in this book. Any omissions will be rectified in subsequent printings if notice is given to the publisher. The paper used to print this book comes from sustainable resources.

Some words are shown in bold, **like this**. They are explained in the glossary on page 24.

Contents

Welcome to the Vet's Office!

This is a vet's office.

People bring animals here for the vet to check.

5

Working as a Vet

I am a vet.

I help sick animals.
I also give **check-ups**
to healthy animals.

What I Wear

In the office I wear a white coat.

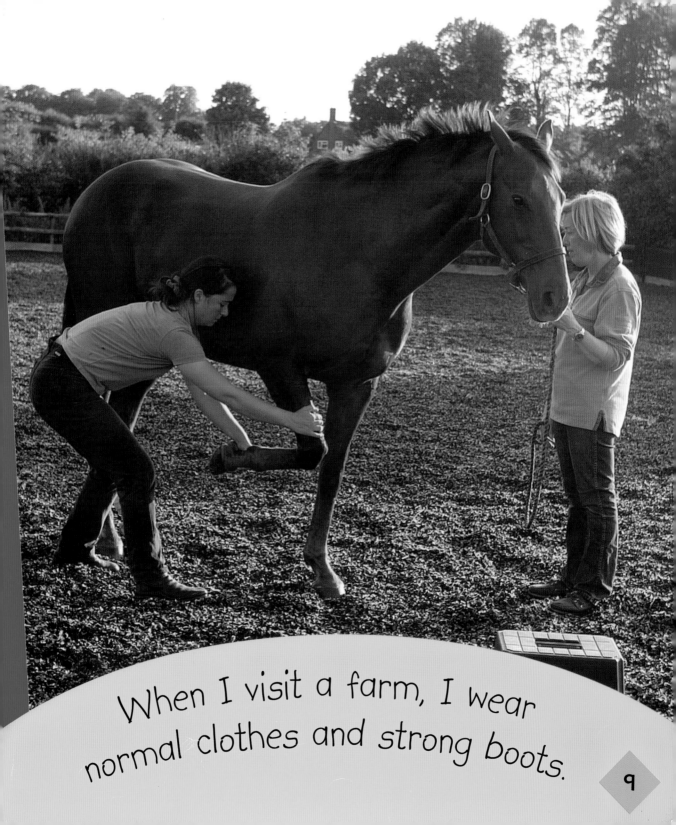

When I visit a farm, I wear normal clothes and strong boots.

An Operation

I wear gloves and special clothes for an **operation**.

They stop **germs** from getting on the animals.

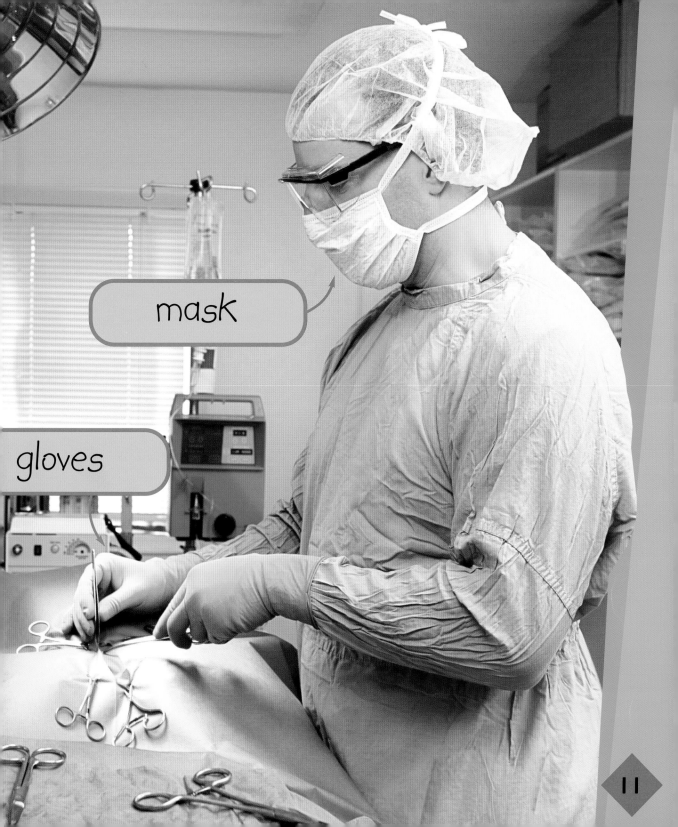

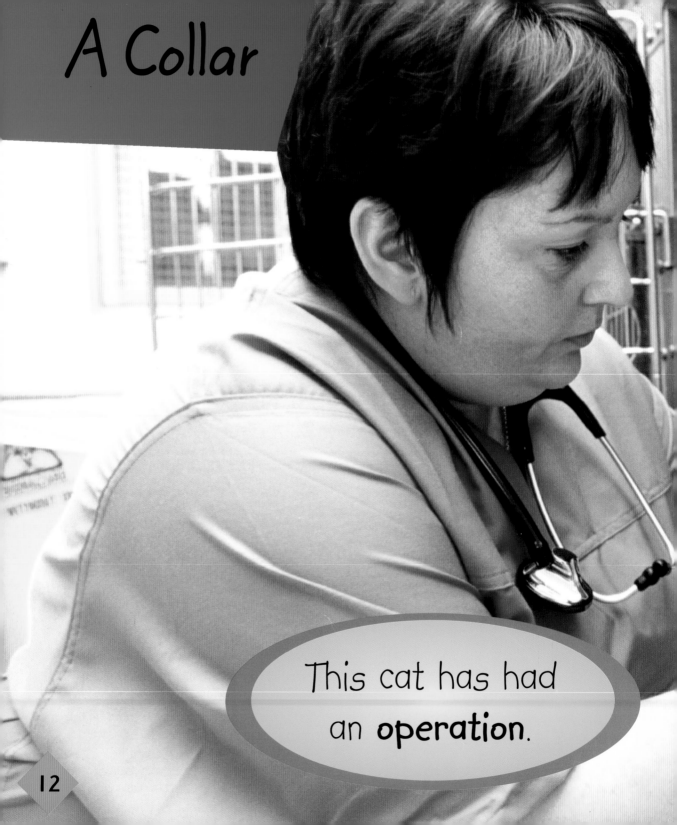

A Collar

This cat has had an **operation**.

The collar stops the cat from licking its **stitches**.

13

Heartbeats

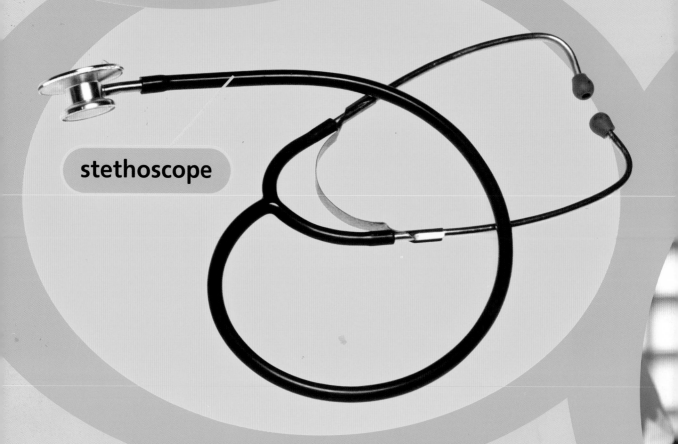

stethoscope

This is my stethoscope.

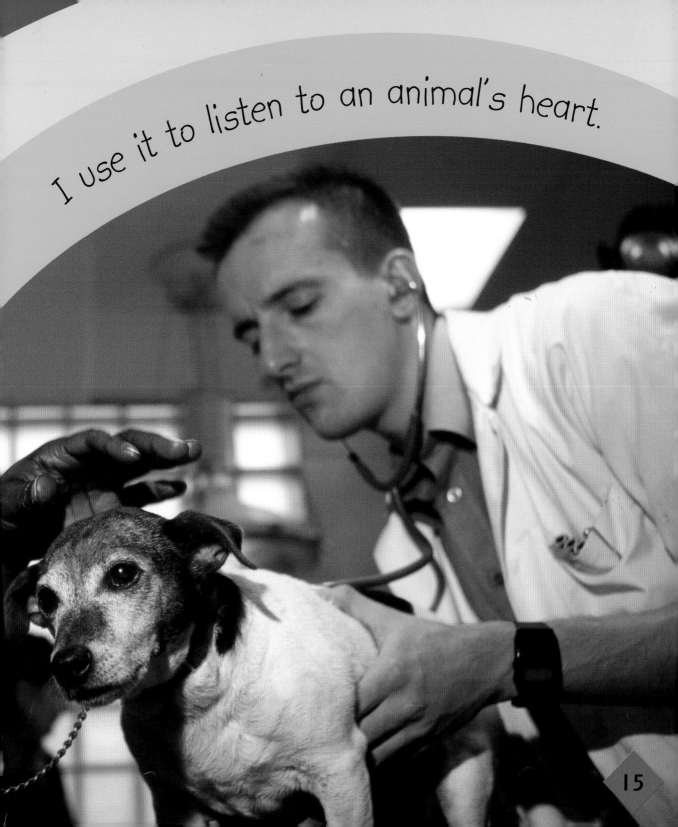

I use it to listen to an animal's heart.

15

I use special **clippers** to cut them.

Visiting a Farm

Sometimes I visit
animals on the farm.

19

Night Time

Some animals have to stay at the vet's over night.

A nurse looks after the animals until the morning.

Quiz

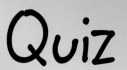

space food

Do you want to be a vet?
Which of these things
would you need?

stethoscope

spacesuit

helmet

22

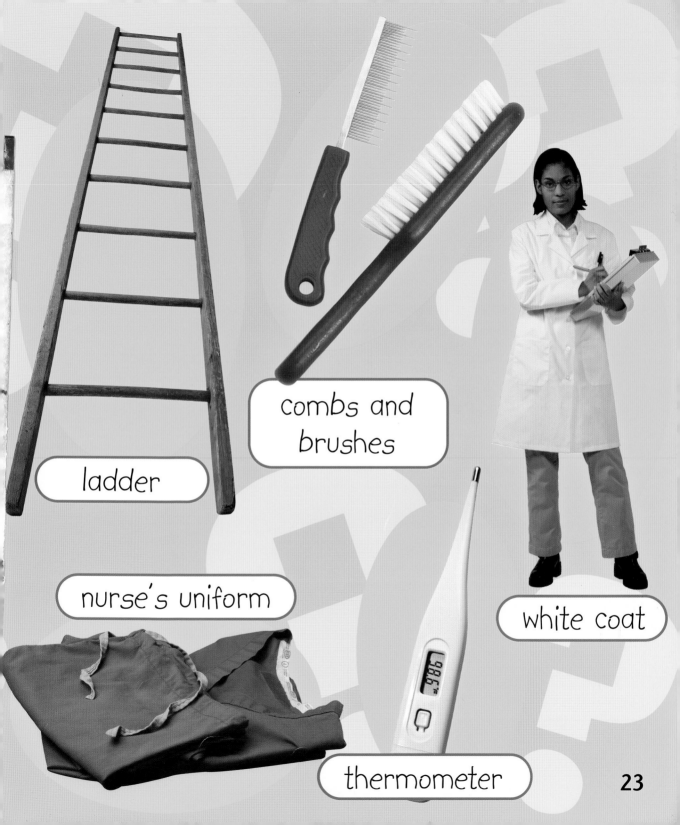

ladder

combs and brushes

nurse's uniform

white coat

thermometer

23

Glossary

check-up visit to the doctor to make sure that you are healthy

clippers special tool for cutting animals' claws

germs things in the air that can make you ill

operation a way of making an animal better

stethoscope what a vet uses to listen to an animal's heartbeat

stitches thread used to sew up a cut

Index

Notes for Adults

This series supports the young child's exploration of their learning environment and their knowledge and understanding of their world.

The series shows the different jobs that professionals do in four different environments. There are opportunities to compare and contrast the jobs and provide an understanding of what each entails.

The books will help the child to extend their vocabulary, as they will hear new words. Some of the words that may be new to them in **We Work at the Vet's** are *check-up, operation, germs, stitches, clippers,* and *stethoscope.* Since the words are used in context in the book this should enable the young child to gradually incorporate them into their own vocabulary.

Follow-up Activities
The child could role play situations in a vet's office. Areas could be set up to create a waiting room, operating room, and cages for in-patients. The child could also record what they have found out by drawing, painting, or tape recording their experiences.